Necessary Affliction

A Blueprint from Pain to Purpose

Tracey Bradley

BK
ROYSTON
Publishing

BK Royston Publishing
Jeffersonville, IN
http://www.bkroystonpublishing.com
bkroystonpublishing@gmail.com

© 2024

Cover Design: Elite Book Covers
Cover Photo: Melanie Cox
Logo Designer: Taylor Archie

ISBN-13: 978-1-963136-14-2

Printed in the United States of America

Table of Contents

Dedication

I give honor and glory to God and dedicate this book back to my Heavenly Father for creating me, to my Lord and Savior Jesus Christ for loving me so much that He died so that I might live eternally with Him, and to the Holy Spirit for transforming my life. I am eternally grateful for your love, faithfulness, and forgiveness. Thank you for knowing me before I was in my mother's womb, choosing me for this assignment, and for never giving up on me. I love you Father God with my heart, mind, soul, and strength!

I honor my mother and father for giving me life. I love you.

I thank my children Melanie and Michael who give me a reason to get up every day, even some days when I didn't want to, and persevere through it all. Thank you for allowing me to proudly wear the title Mom and Mommy.

I thank my beautiful grandchildren Liliana and Miracle, who are my sunshine on a rainy day, and it is my pleasure to be their Granny. Because of them, my heart's desire is to leave an inheritance to my children's children.

I thank my grandmother Janie for introducing me to Jesus and for the example of a Proverbs 31 woman. I will always love you and will see you again one day soon.

I want to thank my "besties": you know who you are. Blood could not make us any closer. Thank you for making me and my life better. I love y'all!

I thank QQ, WDW, BGW for holding me down and allowing me to be my authentic self Always! Your love and friendship mean the world to me. Blood does not make us family, but WE ARE! I love y'all!

I thank my siblings, family, and friends for being a part of my Blueprint. I love y'all!

I thank the She Is Me Ministry, LLC team and everyone who believed in the vision. I appreciate you, and your love and support more than you will ever know. I love y'all.

I thank my church family: R. E. Jones UMC, Canaan Christian Church, Kingdom Fellowship, Bates Memorial, and Ministries of Christ for preaching the gospel of Jesus Christ where I accepted Him as my Lord and Savior and for helping me to learn to trust God, teaching me the foundational, fundamental principles, truths, and precepts of God, and for helping me build my personal relationship with Him, nurturing my gifts, for allowing me the space to grow and serve in ministry, for seeing in me what I did not see in myself, for helping me to accept my calling as a Minister of the Gospel and walk in my purpose. Thank you all for giving me a place to call home, for seeing God in me, and for allowing me to spread my wings and fly!

To God be the Glory!

Foreword

When I first met Tracey, I had already heard a ton about her through my wife. My wife bragged about a person that was loving, genuine, personable, and bubbly just like her. My first encounter with Tracey, I noticed that she had a very kind and gentle spirit. She was going through a divorce, but her spirit was resilient because she acted like a person that was about to get married. Two things that stuck out to me the most about Tracey is first, the fruit that she displayed every time I saw her. Galatians 5: 22-23 (NLT) "But the Holy Spirit produces this kind of fruit in our lives: love, joy, peace, patience, kindness, goodness, faithfulness, gentleness, and self-control. There is no law against these things!"

The second thing that stuck out to me is that she was very easy to talk to. Many people personally came up to me and said that Tracey was a big help to them, and they just love her spirit. I believe this characteristic is so underrated in the body of Christ. Our Savior represents someone that is easy to talk to. Jesus said my yoke is easy and My burden is light. I applaud Tracey on the fact that she allowed her light to shine through even some of the darkest moments in her life. Matthew 5: 14 (NKJV) "You are the light of the world. A city that is set on a hill cannot be hidden.

At our church, the first person that came to mind to help women and counsel them was no other than Tracey. When she told me just some of her life story, I realized that she was the perfect example of an overcomer. Romans 8: 37 (NKJV) "Yet in all these things we are more than conquerors through Him who loved us." There are many women that deal with trauma such as molestation, single parenting, rough marriage, financial hardship, and so much more. Through Tracey's faith in God, she has conquered them all and I know she will help other women realize that **"She Is Me**."

Pastor Vincent Alexander
New Life Ministries of Christ
Louisville, KY

Foreword

Tracey's story is more than a memoir, it's a testimony and a testament. The favor God has on her life is undeniable and her acceptance of it has opened a new door for women everywhere to receive the wisdom God is offering through Tracey's testimony. May the readers of this book be encouraged to keep the faith, no matter what the circumstances look like or the setbacks they encounter. God is faithful and Tracey's memoir is a testament to that truth.

Victoria Carney

President/ Overseer

Ministries of Christ

Louisville, KY

Foreword

Imagine a caterpillar. Unassuming, earthbound, seemingly destined to crawl. Yet, within its unassuming form lies a magnificent truth - the potential for wings, for vibrant colors, for soaring above the limitations of its current existence. The journey to becoming a butterfly is not effortless. It requires a period of seclusion, a transformation hidden from the world. It demands shedding the familiar, dissolving the self it once knew, and embracing the vulnerability of becoming something entirely new.

This is not unlike your journey of healing from trauma. Just as the caterpillar carries the blueprint for wings within its very being, you too hold the potential for a magnificent transformation. Past trauma may have left its mark, etching lines upon your soul like the veins on a butterfly and its wings. But these are not just scars. They are maps – testaments to your strength, resilience, and the incredible journey you've already undertaken.

Remember, the most dazzling butterflies emerge from the most challenging transformations. Just as the chrysalis reveals the hidden beauty within, your journey will unveil the magnificent being you were always meant to be. So spread your wings and take flight. The world awaits the vibrant essence you have to offer.

May this book by the amazing Tracey Bradley, inspire you to fly free. May it help you to embrace the fullness of who you are, nurture the seeds of possibility within you, and to embark on the path towards becoming the very best version of yourself. I am a living testament that Tracey's anointing and ability to equip you on a path of resilience and blossom will change your life. I've watched her go through her very own cocoon and fly free into her purpose, firsthand. She is truly your passionate access to SHE is ME. For just as the butterfly emerges from the cocoon, transformed and renewed, so too shall you emerge from the depths of healing, radiant and whole.

Brandy Nicole
The Healing Princess
Trauma and Behavioral Health Coach
Columbia, SC

Introduction

My story is not a rag-to-riches fairy tale nor is it uncommon, but I believe it does deserve to be told because it is so relatable and identifiable across genders, cultures, and ethnicities. I love God, accepted Jesus Christ as my Lord and Savior, and became a Christian at the age of sixteen years. I grew up in church and use the phrase "born on a pew" often because I do not remember a time in my childhood when I was not in church. My earliest childhood memory of church was singing the songs "This Little Light of Mine" and "He's Got the Whole World in His Hands" in the children's choir. I have been singing in church and gospel choirs ever since. All the singing, serving, praying, and worshipping did not exempt me from the issues of life. In fact, the Bible clearly states, *"I have told you all this so that you may have peace in me. Here on earth, you will have many trials and sorrows. But take heart, because I have overcome the world."* (John 16:33 NLT)

Reading my story from chapter to chapter, many details will be difficult to envision, but my prayer is that through the good, the bad, and the ugly, you will find inspiration and encouragement. My journey has been a testament to determination, perseverance, resiliency, and triumph! After an encounter with God in the latter part of my life, I was finally able to answer the burning question that lies within us all, *"what is my purpose on earth?"* With a new mindset and true identity in Christ, I was able to move beyond my pain. I applied the knowledge, wisdom, and tools that I've acquired over the years from my college education, personal studies, and teachings from biblical scholars, industry experts, and leaders, which propelled me from barely surviving a life of mental and physical anguish to discovering and walking in my purpose. This transformation changed the trajectory of my life, as well as the lives of others.

As I recount the memories of my past, may they inspire you to embrace your own journey of healing and renewal, knowing that by the unconditional love, mercy, and grace of our Heavenly Father, all things are possible. My hope is that you will be empowered to fulfill your destiny and change future generations.

"For I know the plans I have for you," declares the Lord, *"plans to prosper you and not to harm you, plans to give you hope and a future."* (Jeremiah 29:11 NIV)

Chapter 1.

Born in Pain

I came into the world on March 9, 1970, in Louisville, Kentucky, a city steeped in history and nestled along the banks of the Ohio River. My arrival marked the encounter, however brief, of two young souls—my mother, just 19 years old, and my father, 21.

No one ever questions their identity and if their parents are really who they say they are, unless they are given reason to. I never had any reason to believe that it was all a lie and that I had been deceived most of my life. I was always told that I looked just like my daddy and as a young child I believed it. My family would say "you have your daddy's chicken legs" and "you have your daddy's hair" or "you sing just like your daddy" and "you are chocolate just like your daddy." I never knew that none of it was true, although I did suspect as I got older that I was different from the rest of my daddy's family.

I recall as a young child feeling loved by my mother and grandparents. I've always been told that I was a beautiful baby. My favorite aunt would even go as far as to say that I was extraordinarily beautiful. I didn't see that when I looked in the mirror, all I saw was a short chocolate kid with a tiny nose. I remember hearing epithets that stuck with me for life like, "the blacker the berry, the sweeter the juice." Not knowing where it originated, it made me feel special, so I took pride in my dark complexion. In the early years, I believed my family and life were no different from any other during that time. Little did I know the journey ahead would be full of twists and turns, which would shape my identity.

I recall being a loving and affectionate child. Making friends came naturally to me. There was something about the sound of music that soothed my soul, and I began singing in church at an early age. The adventures of books and learning new things excited me. I would choose a letter from the Encyclopedia Brittanica at my grandmother's house and immerse myself for hours. Like most children during the 1970's, I have fond childhood memories of playing outside and in the park with friends and family. My grandmother Janie was very active in church and took all her grandchildren with her as much as possible. I think back to Sunday dinners after church service, vacation Bible school, and summer camp. Not all my recollections from childhood were as pleasant. There were so many others that were not happy at all.

One of the earliest traumatic encounters happened at daycare when I was around the age of four or five. I recall during nap time on the mat while I was supposed to be sleeping, a boy (not sure of his age) came over to me while I was lying on my stomach, and he started rubbing me on my back, buttocks, and down my legs. I lay on the mat as stiff as a board, with my eyes closed and held my breath, as I felt his hand moving across my body. I did not scream or cry; nor did I stop him. At some point, one of the daycare workers saw what was happening and pulled him away from me. When my parents arrived to pick me up, they were told about the issue, and that my behavior was unacceptable. I was suspended from daycare for a while along with the little boy. I remember being reprimanded at home for "letting it happen" and that I must have done something to make the boy touch me and not anyone else. I felt so dirty and ashamed and believed it was my fault even though I didn't fully understand, nor could I articulate what I had just experienced.

Another incident that stands out in my mind as a child was when I was around five years old. I can still see very vividly all our belongings thrown out in the courtyard of the apartment complex after we were evicted from our home. I remember people rummaging through our things as my mother tried to collect as much as she could. I recall my daddy yelling at her to "hurry up" and pick up certain things. Her fear of him is so evident now, but I didn't recognize it at that time.

As a child, my perception of my father was colored by the limited interactions we shared. He was selfish and mean spirited. While I did not spend a lot of time with him growing up even though my parents were married, we did not have a close relationship. Weekends and holidays spent at his mother's house offered rare glimpses of him and I held a sense of respect for him born not out of familiarity or affection, but out of the inherent bond between parent and child. Despite the distance that separated us, I struggled to reconcile my perceptions of him with the idealized image of fatherhood that society showed, which was a figure of strength and guidance, of love and support, whose presence was felt in the lives of his children. And yet, for me, reality fell far short of fantasy, marked by emotional distance and disconnection, by missed opportunities and unspoken words. Growing up, I wrestled with feelings of confusion and resentment over the disconnect between the father I longed for and the father I knew, resentment over the emotional void that was between us.

My dad was raised in a two-parent home and had five brothers and a sister. They were all close. I have sweet memories of my grandparents although there are only a few. What I do recall is love in the home. I loved being there. It was like any other family home and wasn't perfect. I remember some arguments and shouting, even a few fights between the siblings as I suspect most do at some point as youth and young adults. My grandfather died before I reached six years of age and I only have one memory of him. One Saturday morning, he and my grandmother went to visit my uncle in the local jail after shopping at the farmers market downtown. I remember sitting on my grandad's lap as he held the phone on the other side of the glass across from his son. The picture of that moment in time is very clear to me for some reason and is the only memory I have of us together. After my grandfather passed away, my grandmother never remarried. My grandmother lived down the street from her mother and sister so we visited them often and likewise they would do the same. I loved the occasions spent with aunts, uncles, and cousins filled with love, laughter, and lots of food.

I have wonderful memories of my maternal family as well. My mother's parents were married and lived together until my grandmother died from cancer. My grandfather died not long after — they said from a broken heart. They loved and cared for each other very much. My grandmother was a prime example of a Southern woman from Birmingham, Alabama. I believe that's why my southern accent is still so strong today. My heart smiles when I think of her cooking in the kitchen. I can still see her flipping the pineapple upside down cake out of the cast-iron skillet. Sneaking sips of coffee from her mug each morning before my granddaddy walked me to the bus stop was a morning ritual. The most precious memories I have of my granddaddy are the times that I stood in his bed as a young child, while he sat on the edge as I brushed his beautiful hair, which was wavy and black with streaks of silver.

Growing up, I was surrounded by the comforting presence of family gatherings filled with laughter and love, and traditions passed down through the generations. All the while, an absence of visible father-child interactions, of the kind of affectionate gestures and meaningful connections that define the parent-child relationship. For me, the notion of fatherhood was a concept defined more by absence than presence.

Although he was alive and bore the title, my dad's contribution to my life and wellbeing was practically nonexistent. I don't have any fond memories of me together with my parents. I remember that he always drove nice cars, wore nice clothes and a lot of jewelry, and always kept his hair styled, whether it was long, short, or curly. He worked in a cigarette manufacturing factory and always smelled like cigarettes. What made it worse was that he smoked them as well, which is probably why I hate the smell of them to this day.

While my dad and I were not close, I had no reason to conclude that he was not my birth father. God knew what He was doing during the summer of 1969 when He allowed my mother and my biological father to meet, come together — and just for a moment in time — produce me, and never be together again. I didn't know that my DNA was different than my family's but what I did know deep down inside is that I always FELT different. Different from my siblings. Different from my cousins. Different from my friends. I couldn't explain the difference besides the fact that I physically looked different from my family, but I just always felt it inside.

I will go into further detail later in my story.

Although I never got the chance to ask my dad before he passed away from cancer, I now believe that he knew I was not his child. I was told by his sister that my "Daddy" would beat my mother in the stomach and try to kill me while I was still in her womb. God protected me because He knew that I was not a mistake. I was not an accident. God was intentional and used my biological parents to create me, and I was born with purpose. During moments of reflection years later, I began to see my daddy not as a distant figure to be feared or revered, but just as a flawed and imperfect human being, struggling to navigate his life just as I was. And with that realization came a sense of empathy and recognition of our shared humanity that bound us together, despite the barriers that separated us.

"Before I formed you in the womb I knew you, before you were born I set you apart; I appointed you as a prophet to the nations." Jeremiah 1:5 (NIV)

Chapter 2.

Raised in Pain

Growing up as a child, the things that I so often take for granted now were not a part of my reality then. Prior to my parents' divorce, I honestly cannot remember a time when we were all together as a family. As the winds of change swept through our lives, carrying us toward an uncertain future, the foundations of my childhood began to crumble when we moved from the stable home of my mother's parents when I was in the fifth grade.

As I stepped into a new elementary school, the landscape of my world underwent a subtle yet seismic shift that would change the contours of my existence in a profound way. While my mom was forced to become independent, there was always a shadow of her silent struggle. For my mother, the absence of a driver's license was not a barrier, but a testament to her resilience and ingenuity. We settled into our new home on the south side of town, where I found myself enveloped in a world of possibility in which convenience and accessibility were not luxuries, but necessities of daily living. With the school just across the street, my daily commute became a ritual of familiarity and our family lived in that area until I entered high school.

Discovering a strength and determination that she did not realize she had, my mom worked at what was then known as General Hospital in the registration department of the emergency room on the third shift from eleven o'clock at night until seven o'clock in the morning. This shift afforded her the ability to work a full-time job as we slept through the night to avoid the added pressure of childcare payments, and there were times when my older cousin would babysit to help her as well. Working long hours and sacrificing her own needs in pursuit of a better life for her children, my mom still struggled in the face of poverty. As she navigated the unchartered waters of being a single parent of three young children, as a young, poor, black woman with only a high school education in the seventies and eighties, it was nearly impossible for her to get ahead alone. She strived to feed us, clothe us, and pay the bills. I know she did the best she could with what she had, but she always made it clear that no one was to ever know what went on inside her home. And we made sure no one ever did.

Mental illness, like an uninvited guest, began to take up residence within our home. I was unaware at that time that there were signs to look for even though they were right in front of my face. As a child, mental illness was never spoken of in our family although it was apparent in multiple households including my own. The novella *The Strange Case of Dr. Jekyll and Mr. Hyde* was a horror story written by Robert Louis Stevenson in 1886. The book, based in London, England, in 1887, tells the story of Dr. Henry Jekyll who performs experiments with a serum that he believes will separate the good and evil intentions of people. When the doctor takes his own serum, it causes Mr. Hyde, his alter ego, to be born. His face becomes disfigured, and his voice is unrecognizable to those who know him. The personalities of Dr. Jekyll and Mr. Hyde are completely different. Jekyll is a kind and respectful doctor, although determined in his venture to prove his theories. Mr. Hyde, on the other hand, is evil and violent with no concern for anyone but himself.

Having seen some parts of the American movie version, *Dr. Jekyll and Mr. Hyde,* I would often compare my mother's behavior with both characters. Most of the time, she, like Dr. Jekyll, was mild mannered and even funny, but she would flip like a light switch and become someone completely different in an instant with an evil tone, someone mean spirited using foul language, and someone with contorted facial expressions. I would literally run to my room, lock the door, saying to myself, "my mother is Dr. Jekyll and Mr. Hyde," because I had no clinical language to describe it and that was the only point of reference, I had to compare what I had just witnessed. I really did not understand what was happening right in front of me, but it happened so often that I just learned to live with it. The change not only began to happen more frequently, but she became more violent. The physical beatings were a regular part of my childhood in middle school with physical scars that have healed but are still visible to this day.

The mother that I had known began to disappear right before my very eyes. Multiple personalities, like fragmented mirrors reflecting fractured truths, wove a tapestry of complexity that defied comprehension. In her moments of clarity, she was warm, caring, and had a great sense of humor. Yet the reality of schizophrenia set in with each passing day, and the veil of sanity grew thinner. My mom's depression, like a relentless tide, engulfed her spirit and was a suffocating weight that pressed down on her soul. And yet, between the chaos and confusion, there were moments of joy that transcended the boundaries of illness and despair. In her laughter, however temporary, and in her embrace, however fragile, I found peace, a reminder that in the middle of the storm, there existed pockets of tranquility, however short lived.

Amid the turmoil, I became a reluctant observer and a witness to the ebb and flow of a tide I could neither calm nor understand. Not only did my mother's mental condition become worse, but her financial state did also. As she suffered, it became increasingly difficult to keep the lights on, water running, and food on the table. When the water was off, while everyone else was asleep, my little brother and I would take a bucket and go to the neighbors' outdoor water spigot at night in the dark to fill it up. We would all use the same water to wash our bodies before bed.

Our electricity was off more than it was on. My imagination and passion for storytelling blossomed during those times because we could not watch television. I read books from the library, newspapers, and magazines that would give me an alternate reality from what I was experiencing. My reading skills had surpassed most of my peers and I rocketed to a high school level before I completed elementary school. A fascination with the news developed during those times and by high school I dreamt of a day when it would be me reporting the evening news. The contrast between the challenges of home life during the week and the warmth and comfort of weekends spent at my grandmother's house often left me counting down the days until the arrival of the weekend. From the moment I stepped through the door, I felt the weight of the week melt away and the burdens of responsibility giving way to the simple joys of family connection and laughter.

My mother had engrained in me that what happened in her house stayed in her house, so no one ever knew the conditions we were living in. The cloak of shame that shrouded our family's struggles with our mother's mental illness and the accompanying hardships cast a long shadow over our upbringing, complicating the already difficult journey of me and my siblings. In the veil of silence that blanketed our home and disguised our struggles in secrecy, the weight of humiliation hung heavy. Behind closed doors, we bore witness to the demon of my mother's silent battles of mental illness, a burden she carried in seclusion. Yet, the walls of our home held more than just the echoes of her delusional beliefs; they held the weight of our isolation.

In the eyes of the world, we wore masks of normalcy, a facade carefully crafted to shield us from the looks and questions of our neighbors and friends. Behind smiles, we concealed the scars of our reality: a truth marked by hardship, hunger, and the unrelenting grip of embarrassment. To speak of our struggles was to invite scrutiny, a risk too great to bear. Our voices and pain had been silenced by the societal stigma.

No one ever saw the physical scars from beatings I received during my mother's psychotic episodes because I wore long sleeves — even during the summer. When we got to my grandmother's house, it was such a relief to be around my cousins and just be normal without the worry or responsibility of having to care for my younger siblings. I could appreciate the things that we so often take for granted like turning on the faucet with running water to brush my teeth, take a bath, or watch the "Love Boat" on TV. To go to the refrigerator to get cold milk for a bowl of cereal was a treat. These were weekend privileges for me that I longed for Monday through Friday.

So, you can imagine, for any child, the older I got the more I desired a sense of normalcy like my peers. By my 8th grade year, I had a lot of friends in my neighborhood. Even though our lifestyle inside the home had not changed, my personality had. Becoming popular and likeable in school, I learned early on how to live a double life so that none of my friends ever suspected there was trouble at home until one day.

On a hot summer night, the power went out in the neighborhood, and everything went dark, except our unit was lit up from the outside looking in. Unbeknownst to our neighbors, our home was lit by candlelight at night quite often because we were without electricity. It never occurred to us that the power was out for everyone else. So, one of the neighbors came over to talk to my mother while I was on the porch with a friend to ask why our power was not out like everyone else's, but she had already gone to work for the night. That same neighbor made a point to come back the next day to discuss the power outage with my mother while I was at school. When I came home, I was immediately met with a beating because now the neighbors knew that we had no electricity before the power outage. Now all the neighbors knew her business and it was all my fault because if I had not been outside after she went to work no one would have been the wiser. Oh, was I in trouble! It was the worst beating of my life, and I did not think I was going to survive. After what seemed like an eternity from each blow that I received, she took a break and retreated to her room, but not before announcing that she was going to kill me that night — and I believed her. After hearing the creak of her bedroom door closing, I knew I had to escape. I climbed out of my second-floor bedroom window and jumped down to the ground but consequently sprained my ankle trying to break my fall. I managed to hobble to a friend's house and asked them to call my dad to save me. As they looked on in horror at the blood, bruises, and whelps that I had sustained, my friend's mother managed to clean my wounds and bandage me up. When my father arrived, I explained what had just occurred and why. He decided that the best course of action would be to return me to my mother so that I could apologize for embarrassing them both and putting others in their business. Gripped in fear and dismay, it was inconceivable that my father would drive me back home and drop me off at my mother's doorstep, but he did just that. I thought my life was over at that point, but my mother told me that she was not going to touch me again that night since other people had already seen me. And so, I lived to see another day.

High school, a time meant for growth and learning, became a battleground where the demands of home surpassed the pursuit of education. Days blurred into nights. My mother's absence became my burden. She spent more of her days and nights at her new boyfriend's home than she did at her own. We would go days without seeing her. With my little brother being so young and not in daycare, I had no choice but to be his caregiver, when my mother went missing for days on end. And so, school became a casualty of circumstance, duty, and sacrifices made in the name of family obligation. Each missed day echoed the sound of missed opportunities, of dreams deferred in the wake of necessity. At times I found peace and safety in the embrace of understanding teachers, compassionate classmates, and boys who made me feel good about myself and gave me the attention that I so desperately desired.

Seeking escape and comfort, I leaned toward the affections of boys who showed any sign of interest in me. Not having a sense of self-worth or self-love, not knowing my value or the meaning of it at the time, I accepted the mistreatment of others believing that it was better than not having any connection at all. I had never felt more worthless than the night after a ball game when I got in the car with friends to go home. I sat in the backseat beside another and was the last person in the car. When we got to my grandmother's house, parked right across the street, the friend driving said he wanted to talk to me about something. He opened his door and before I knew it, he was in the back seat with me. As he began to tell me how much he liked me but was afraid to tell me, he finally had the chance. When I expressed that I didn't feel the same way, he then said how disappointed he was and asked for a hug as consolation for being let down. Had I known what was going to happen next, I would never have accepted his offer to take me home. I couldn't explain the seemingly instant wave of fear that came over me. Before I could deny his request, he reached his arm across my chest and pulled me into him. As I pushed away, he then used both arms to push me back into the seat and climbed on top of me. With the strength that I had in the confined space I was in, I tried with all my might to push the six foot, over two-hundred-pound football player off me. To no avail, I lost in my struggle to avoid the rape that occurred that night directly across the street from my place of safety. That secret stayed in my heart and head and yet buried so deep covered with imitation smiles and laughter in the school halls that no one would notice the pain in my eyes.

At 16, I began to stay with my grandmother more frequently during the school year because my mother did not have the means to prepare me for prom and graduation. My life finally began to resemble that of the average teenager. I went to ball games, sang in the school gospel choir, auditioned and was selected to star in a musical in the Youth Performing Arts School where I majored in vocal music. I won a talent show and was even crowned homecoming queen. By my seventeenth birthday and excited about the upcoming junior prom, my future looked bright and promising. While I had my fair share of boy crushes and first dates from my freshman to junior year, only one young man swept me off my feet and took my breath away. He was very handsome, intelligent, charming, and older. Attending the university across the street from my school as a college freshman, I felt like a princess when he would pick me up from high school with my friends looking on in envy. In his presence I felt safe and protected. A feeling that I had longed for but never experienced from a man in my life. He knew just what to say to make all my troubles disappear. It didn't take long for me to fall head over heels. I wanted to spend every waking moment with him. I finally felt the feeling that I had longed for — this must be love, right?

It was a whirlwind romance, and I was living my very own fairy tale. For the first time in my life, I had something that was just for me, and I was happy. The sound of his voice and the smell of his cologne lingered in my mind long after he would leave my presence and hold me until we could be together again. I began to spend my days, nights, and weekends with him, all the while informing my grandmother that I was with a best friend. After months of dating, what was once elation turned to dread. Each morning began the same way with waves of nausea and vomiting, so I knew something must be wrong. I ate soup and crackers thinking it was just a virus, but nothing eased the discomfort and illness. After going to the doctor and having to reconcile the very real fact that I was now going to be a teenage mother, I became overwhelmed with a myriad of emotions. Not wanting to be a disappointment and failure to my very religious grandmother, I felt that I couldn't tell the one person who truly loved and supported me unconditionally. When I finally gathered the strength to tell the father of my baby that I was carrying his child, he not only declared that the baby wasn't his but accused me of sleeping with someone else and broke off our relationship. I was completely and utterly devastated. With no hope and no support, I believed I had no choice but to end the pregnancy. I can still envision me sitting in the waiting room of the clinic, with a feeling of bewilderment and sorrow as the nurse called my name. Taking her hand and walking through those doors is a memory that I will never forget. Returning to school to finish my senior year and carrying an unspeakable secret as well as the residue of guilt and shame from my decision, felt unbearable at times. I found inner strength through prayer and my faith in God even at a young age, believing that he saw my tears, and felt my pain. There were many bouts of depression as I cried out silently in mental anguish, but it was the Lord that carried me forward. By the grace of God and help from my grandmother, I was able to attend the senior prom and finish my senior year, graduating in May of 1988. In the summer of that same year, my mother had been evicted from her apartment again and moved in with her new boyfriend. The physical abuse was evident. She was a prisoner of her own fear and held hostage by his words and actions. I witnessed the toll that he exacted on her when she called me to pick her up from the hospital and police station on more than one occasion. I tried to convince her to leave him, but fear held her in its grip, casting a shadow over her hopes and dreams, suffocating the light of her spirit with its oppressive weight. She believed she had no place to go, and she forbade me to tell anyone.

One December afternoon in 1988, was a day etched in time and a chapter of my life stained with the blood of innocence lost. I went to my mother's boyfriend's apartment to visit my younger sister and little brother. He was four years old. I was stopped outside the door by police and EMS workers and was told that I could not enter the building which had caution tape roped around it, and I was turned away. Later that evening, when I returned home, I was met by several family members saddened and weeping.

I was clueless to what was happening around me. My grandmother mustered the strength and proceeded to tell me that my little brother had been murdered by my mother's boyfriend earlier that day. I was devastated. Overcome with grief, I remember whaling in agony. My heart was broken. How could something so evil happen to someone so innocent?

In the aftermath of tragedy, a courtroom drama played out against the backdrop of our shattered lives. The prosecutor showed that my brother's murder was the worst case of violence and torture that our county had seen. The grief and anguish from my brother's death was unbearable at times. To escape the pain, I found myself sleeping through days at a time so that I would not have to replay it over again in my mind and accept the reality that he was really gone. The anger and hatred that raged inside me was unlike anything I had ever felt before, and I had no comprehension of how to deal with it.

After I testified against my mother and her boyfriend in the criminal trial, they were both convicted and sentenced to prison. He was ordered to serve a life sentence behind bars in prison for murder, and she for neglect and accessory to murder. Their fates were sealed by the weight of their actions, but the verdict offered little solace in the face of irreparable loss.

In the aftermath of my brother's murder, the weight of grief hung heavy in the air. In her desperation to make sense of the senselessness, my mother turned to blame, casting me as the fall guy in the tragedy. In her eyes, I was not just a grieving sibling, but a guilty accomplice whose actions had led to my brother's death, believing had I not left home to stay with my grandmother, he would still be alive. And try as I might to shake off the shackles of guilt, I found myself unable to escape the shadow of her accusations.

For months, I grappled with the demons of guilt and self-loathing. The burden of guilt and the emotional trauma inflicted by my mother's accusations cast a shadow over my grieving process. I underwent months of therapy to overcome the guilt that my mother forced upon me. As much as I tried to forgive her and see the mother whom I once loved and respected, only anger and resentment filled my heart for many years. Through prayer, the word of God, therapy, and the love and support of family, I was able to forgive those who harmed me and release the burdens that had weighed me down for so long.

"[Cast] all your cares [all your anxieties, all your worries, and all your concerns, once and for all] on Him, for he cares about you [with deepest affection, and watches over you very carefully]." 1 Peter 5:7 (AMP)

Chapter 3.

Married to Pain

In the wake of my high school trauma, I found a sense of compassion and comfort in the arms of a familiar friend. His father being the pastor of my grandmother's church, we grew close during our teenage years. But the summer after graduation would tear us apart as he left to pursue higher education; I stayed behind, enrolling in community college. I soon found myself ensnared in the embrace of a new relationship that promised love but delivered little more than heartache and a union forged in desperation, in longing, in the fleeting promise of escape. I often wondered what turn of events would have taken place had I waited for his return.

I met my first husband in September of 1988. We were attending the same college party. As it happened, we were both riding in the car with our friends who were beside each other in the parking lot. While his friend was engaged in conversation with my friend, we locked eyes with each other, then a smile, and the rest is history for the next eighteen years.

He was a man of contradictions, full of charm and charisma yet haunted by the demons that lurked beneath the surface. His words were honeyed lies, dripping with deceit causing a web of half-truths and broken promises that led only to despair. Alcohol was his refuge and his poison. Wanting a fresh start in my new-found freedom as an adult, I needed to leave the trauma of my past behind. By December of that year, I found myself pregnant with my son. Religion ruled our home and gauged my grandmother's response when I told her I was going to be a mother. Her response was not what I expected, in light of the fact that I hardly knew the father. She said that I had to get married to make it right with God and because *"I made my bed, now I had to lie in it."* What a sobering thought!

My soon to be husband had also been raised in the church, however he had God nowhere on his mind. His father, however, had the same response as my grandmother. So, bypassing all the red warning signs of alcoholism, narcissism, low-self-esteem, and unresolved childhood trauma of his own, this man would become my husband by October of the very next year.

By the age of twenty, I now had a son and daughter, who was born just thirteen months later. I was also the wife of an alcoholic husband who had enlisted in the Army and moved me and my children away from everything I had known. I now had to learn to adapt to a new way of life in Columbus, Georgia, stationed at Ft. Benning as an army wife and mother of a toddler and newborn. It was amidst the backdrop of barracks and training grounds that the seeds of our family's future took root — a future marked by the arrival of new life, new beginnings, and new challenges.

As my husband answered the call to duty, I stood by his side, a silent witness to the rhythms of military life that beat like a steady drum in the distance. My example of a wife and mother was shaped by my dad's mother. While I had a great relationship with my mother's parents who were married and lived together until their passing, and I had spent a lot of time with my maternal cousins, aunts and uncles who were all very close, but it was my Grandmother Janie who was everything that I aspired to be. College educated, well spoken, well respected, intelligent, classy, elegant, poised, compassionate, kind, loving, and a faith-filled woman of God who introduced me to Jesus Christ. Because of her love of traveling across the country and always bringing back stories of her adventures, I am now an avid traveler. As a compassionate public-school teacher and church women's ministry leader, she made a difference in the lives of others. She also sang in the church choir and taught Sunday school. She was indeed my she-ro!

And so, as I embarked on a journey of self-discovery, it became a journey marked by trials and triumphs, as well as heartache and healing. Now, on my own, in a new role, I would live the next thirty-plus years attempting to follow in my grandmother's footsteps to earn her respect, approval, and admiration. As I settled into motherhood and becoming a housewife, I learned very quickly that it was not as easy as it appeared. While watching the television shows "I love Lucy" and "The Jeffersons" the wives always looked perfect with not a hair out of place, always wearing a dress and heels, all while cooking, cleaning and taking care of a child. It didn't take me long to realize that it was not reality. Being away from my support system, I knew nothing about raising two small children. Becoming pregnant with my daughter just four months after giving birth to my son didn't allow much time to learn the basics of motherhood. Talk about winging it! It was on-the-job training for sure. Using cloth diapers and my own breast milk proved cost effective and convenient rather than buying pampers and formula and warming bottles in the middle of the night. With my husband at the bottom of the military totem pole and me not having a job, to say that we struggled financially is an understatement. A small metal box in a mobile home park is what we called home. Our meal of choice was Hamburger Helper, and birthday celebrations consisted of a simple box of Jiffy cake mix and canned icing.

In the year 1990, my husband answered the call of duty that beckoned him to the sands of the Middle East. I clung to memories. Each letter and the sound of his voice on each call, became a lifeline that bridged the distance, connecting us across the oceans. In the embrace of fellow military families bound by a common purpose, I found comfort and strength.

As the sound of the conflict faded into the distance, replaced by the silence of uneasy peace, my husband returned home as a soldier transformed by the war. His spirit had been scarred by the indelible marks of trauma and turmoil. The Gulf War had left its imprint upon him, a shadow that lingered in the depths of his being. PTSD became more than just an acronym. It haunted our days and nights, a silent witness to the unraveling of a soul wounded by the horrors of war. In his eyes, I saw the distant battles, the flash of gunfire, and the cries of comrades. Alcohol became a numbing agent that dulled the edges of his pain.

After receiving orders for the next duty station, we were relocated to serve a four-year tour in Europe where things took a turn for the worse. The move to Heidelberg, Germany, marked a new chapter in our family's journey, filled with unforeseen challenges and trials that tested the limits of endurance and resilience. As the wheels of change set in motion, carrying us across oceans and continents, a cocktail of emotions was as potent as it was unpredictable. Amidst the cobblestone streets and centuries-old architecture, we found ourselves enveloped in a world both foreign and familiar.

My husband's drinking became worse than ever before. In Heidelberg, the fractures within our family deepened, their roots entwined with the complexities of military life and the burdens of duty. The distance from home became more than just a physical separation, it became a void that stretched across oceans, dividing us from the comforts of familiarity and the embrace of loved ones left behind.

The intensity of his drinking caused his temper to escalate as well. On one occasion I attempted to take the car keys from him to prevent him from driving. The rage that followed was so frightening that he almost broke my arm trying to pry them away from me. He struggled to adjust to the new environment and spiraled down a dark hole turning to marijuana along with the increased alcohol consumption. With a failed drug test and mandatory treatment, he made the decision to leave the army.

I must admit, while my marriage was in chaos, the only thing that saved me was my relationship with the Lord. Because God was my foundation and I was still trying to imitate my grandmother, I began going with a co-worker to a non-denominational Christian church. I took my children with me every Sunday and soon became active, teaching Sunday school. Being raised in a United Methodist Church, this was a whole new experience for me. I loved the praise and worship music with drums and a guitar. I had never seen healing services with the laying of hands nor people speaking in tongues. As I wanted more of this new religious experience and began to grow spiritually, I hungered for more. I will never forget the day that changed my spiritual life forever. There was a prayer meeting and we lay before the Lord seeking His presence.

As I prayed for the indwelling of the Holy Spirit, I was given the gift of speaking tongues (an unknown prayer language). It was an experience that I still can't fully articulate, but I know was real. My new relationship with God gave me the strength to cope with my husband until we were discharged from the military and returned home to the United States.

The return home to Kentucky in 1995 marked a pivotal moment of transition and reflection for my family. A return to familiar shores after navigating the tumultuous waters of military life abroad. The return to the U.S. marked the end of one chapter and the beginning of another. For us, coming home was more than just a physical transition, but reclaiming everything that we once knew. Back with family and friends, I had a support system to go to during times of conflict as I tried to hold up my husband as he made the transition back to civilian life. With our children now in school, I began to live the life that I had always dreamed of. We were able to purchase our first home with a VA loan. My husband continued to work for the federal government as a United States Postal Clerk and then shortly thereafter enrolled in school to follow his dream of becoming self employed as a barber. I began my career at United Parcel Service, and I found a church home where I served in ministry teaching young women and singing in the choir. We were able to provide a stable life for our children and they were surrounded by love. They were afforded the freedom to participate in whatever sport or activity of their choosing, which included baseball, football, basketball, cheerleading, dance, and art, as well as community and church youth groups. We had a very busy social life and we appeared to be one big happy family. What no one saw was the trauma that was being perpetrated behind closed doors from the scars of war and the trials of military life abroad. As we settled into the rhythms of civilian existence, the wounds of the past remained ever-present. They were a constant reminder of the sacrifices made and the challenges overcome. My husband continued to fight his demons from the war and unresolved apparent childhood trauma from neglect and unforgiveness after his parents' divorce and relationships with new partners. Those wounds that were never healed began to resurface and infect our environment and the relationships in our home.

Over the years, he began to spiral even further. The ongoing battle that he faced with alcoholism, depression, and PTSD paints a picture of the enduring impact of trauma. His drinking became progressively worse, manifesting in every area and relationship of his life, especially our marriage. The attraction of pornography began to infiltrate our bedroom. The natural desire for sexual interaction between husband and wife slowly disappeared as his hunger for constant sexual gratification was fulfilled. He no longer craved the touch of his wife but would rather masturbate to the pornographic images while lying in the bed right beside me. The atmosphere in our home was filled with hostility from each member of the family and we were all suffering in our own way. The energy would immediately shift from joy to gloom when he came home. His anger and mean-spirited temper would cause the children to go to their rooms to avoid being near him. Feelings of discontent and bitterness began to shape the jaded perception of my marriage. My cynical attitude bled over into every conversation. The constant feeling of sadness weighed heavy, often leading to thoughts of suicide, however brief in the moment.

I began to sense that there was a dark presence in our home. Surviving my day-to-day existence, the stress of my homeless, crack-addicted mother, who had been released from prison, weighed heavily upon my shoulders. The devastating impact of substance abuse posed profound challenges for our family. As my mother fell deeper into the abyss of addiction, the fabric of our family began to unravel. The healing that had taken place in my heart over the years through therapy and my relationship with God, afforded me the ability to foster forgiveness. So, when I received calls for assistance from her, I did what any child would do for their parent, and ran to her aid, providing money, food, clothing, and shelter, even bringing her into our home at times. The revelation that my mother was a drug addict took me to a realm that I never knew existed. I found myself in a spiritual battle of demonic forces. I can recall the very real experience of seeing and feeling an evil spirit on top of my body strangling me, while I was lying in bed next to my husband one night. I began to scream and call on the name of Jesus Christ and the spirit left me. When I woke up my husband, still visibly shaken and in tears, I told him what had just happened to me. He said I was just dreaming, and no one was in the house. He rolled over and went back to sleep. I will never forget that experience for as long as I live.

Over the course of several years, I had survived several encounters with death, the first being while still in Germany. I went into surgery for what should have been a simple procedure to have all four of my wisdom teeth removed. However, I would be moved to intensive care with fluid in my lungs and put on a ventilator for days before being released. The chaplain was called in to pray with my husband because he said at one point the doctors didn't think I would make it. I survived by God's grace. BUT GOD! A near fatal car incident occurred while I was driving down the street one day when my brakes suddenly went out in the car. I lost control, ran through several lights, crossing multiple lanes attempting to avoid colliding with other cars. So afraid that I was going to kill someone or be killed, I remember crying out to God, and finding the presence of mind to steer the car off the road and into a ditch. The car finally came to an abrupt stop, hitting a light pole instead of the brick wall behind the pole. I survived by God's grace. BUT GOD!

On a snowy/icy drive to work one morning, on the interstate, I hit a patch of ice, and the car began spinning out of control. I called out to God, pleading with the Lord to protect the cars around me so that I don't hurt anyone. When the car stopped moving, it was facing the opposite direction, and I was looking at oncoming traffic. I gripped the steering wheel and held on for dear life, shaking in terror and praying that no one would hit me. Miraculously, all the cars heading in my direction managed to avoid crashing into me and I was able to turn the car around in the right direction. When I made it to the off-ramp I slid, hit the guard rail, and the car would not move. I was paralyzed in fear and had given up trying, so I just sat there weeping and praying to God for help me. It was like an out of body experience because while my hands covered my face as I sat crying, the car was suddenly being pushed up the ramp to the top of the hill until I was on the street and when I looked up, I didn't see anything or anyone. I still can't explain it until this day, except it was a miracle from an angel. I survived by God's grace. BUT GOD!

I left the dentist office one afternoon after having a tooth extracted, and I was still under the effects of the nitrous oxide. Apparently falling asleep while driving on the interstate, I woke up and opened my eyes to see that I was in the emergency lane. Still coasting under 5 miles an hour and remarkably, I had not hit anyone, and no one had hit me. I became coherent enough to make it home safely. I survived by God's grace! BUT GOD!

By year sixteen of our marriage, I was suffering from stress, anxiety, suicidal thoughts, depression, and had ballooned to 280 pounds searching for a semblance of comfort through food. As I studied my grandmother while I was growing up and learning to imitate her, the most important yet unintentional lesson she taught me was to always appear to be happy because you are blessed. Even taking a lesson from the times of living with my mother, I would never let anyone know what is going on in my home. So, while I was still going to work every day, serving at church, fulfilling my commitments, and taking care of my children, I felt like I was slowly dying inside and just wanted the pain to end, and often contemplated how I could make it stop forever. Looking back, the slow death internally manifested externally, with even my skin aging and my complexion darkening.

I began to keep myself busy and away from home so that I wouldn't have to deal with the truth of my marriage disintegrating. There was such anxiety during our times of sexual interaction that buried memories of molestation began to resurface. I had submerged the trauma of being abused as a young child by an uncle to the deepest part of my subconscious. The flashbacks became more than just memories — they became portals to my past steeped in darkness. My body would involuntarily become tense when I felt his skin against mine. I literally held my breath and closed my eyes, waiting for the act to end. I could not tolerate my husband's touch any longer. I sought counseling at church, but this changed nothing. As a matter of fact, it made things worse.

The constant arguing persisted until we eventually stopped sharing a bed and he began sleeping in the living room on the sofa. No matter what I did to survive, even working two jobs to help alleviate our financial problems, nothing helped our situation. His wounds and addiction bled into our finances causing our utilities to be cut off and our cars to be repossessed, eventually leading to the foreclosure of the house in the end. By the end of our relationship, I felt as though I was a single parent. The sight of him stressed me out, and his scent made me sick to my stomach. I resented him and carried my bitterness toward him into every conversation we had. I suffered in silence, not sharing my pain with anyone outside our home. I tried to protect my children by shielding them and hiding the truth of my pain from them. I would cover my face with a pillow in the bed and cry in the shower so they would not see or hear me. Deciding after counseling and much prayer to file for divorce, I was able to save enough money to move out of the house that next year. Even though it was the best thing for me and my sanity, I didn't realize that decision would cause so much pain and turmoil for my son that wasn't addressed until years later. While my husband caused me much mental and emotional pain, I always knew it was because of his own unresolved trauma that he refused to address. Hurt people really do hurt people. The Lord eventually gave me the strength and grace to see his actions and behavior for what it really was, and I continue to pray for him.

"But the Lord is faithful, and he will strengthen you and protect you from the evil one." 2 Thessalonians 3:3 (NIV)

Chapter 4.

Hiding in Pain

In the wake of heartache and loss, I sought to
acquire peace now more than ever before and protect it at
all costs. Filled with anticipation, I forged ahead navigating
the waters of my new beginning and journey to the next
chapter of my life. In making preparation for the move to
my new home, I spoke with a fellow church member whom
I had been acquainted with for years and inquired about
assisting me. I had previous knowledge of his feelings
toward me, and I must admit that I presumed that his
answer would be yes. And it was! He later disclosed that he
used a sick day at work because he believed that he would
never get the chance to be with me alone outside of church,
and he was correct. After the move, we continued to talk, as
he would inquire about my progress of getting settled into
my new home. In the quiet corners of my heart, I found

myself vulnerable and drawn to the familiarity of companionship. He became a close friend and confidant in my times of need, a source of laughter and camaraderie during life's trials.

We discovered that we had a lot in common. His sense of humor, personality and love of music kept us engaged for hours on end. Our backgrounds and childhoods were similar as well, both being raised in the church by our grandmothers. He made himself available to me and my children and helped in any way he could. I had never seen this side of him before during our encounters at church. Always kind and courteous, he was a perfect gentleman, never forcing himself or making me feel uncomfortable. I found myself opening to him without apprehension and letting my guard down. I recall one day after he called to inquire if I needed anything, I informed him that I needed some assistance hanging my curtains. When he arrived, he had an ironing board in hand because he said he noticed that I didn't have one. Wow — observant, thoughtful, and selfless. He scored major points that day, which was the beginning of a beautiful friendship.

Amidst the warmth of our shared connection, a longing stirred. A longing for something more, something deeper than mere friendship could provide. In the heady rush of emotions, the line between friendship and romance blurred. A kaleidoscope of longing and desire, of hope and uncertainty. And so it was, in the throes of a rebound, I gave in to my need to feel loved again, despite the echoes of past heartaches. Little did I know at that time that his goal was marriage. After my divorce was final, we began dating and I would become his wife just three years later.

It was a beautiful love story in the beginning. We were inseparable, even dressing alike everywhere we went. Our relationship was a perfect portrait of love. The hues and highlights of support, laughter, and passion held us together. Our children could feel the love between us as we attempted to create a family bond. With my daughter going off to college and my son living with his father, I dreamt of what it would be like to finally be free of the obligation to take care of everyone else and just enjoy life. And yet the trauma from divorce and the pain it caused my son affected my new relationship in ways that I never expected. The tension between them became so thick that it eventually boiled over and erupted into a physical altercation. Looking back in retrospect, I believe had I ended the relationship at that point, it would have saved me from later heartache and pain years later. However, the expectation of my independence outweighed the feeling of mental and emotional exhaustion from my son's behavior over the years and memories of my past. Moving forward meant that I could finally have a life for myself and not carry the weight of responsibility but instead have someone else meet all my wants and needs. So, I chose the latter.

But as the weeks turned into months, and the months into years, the cracks in our foundation began to show — a testament to the fragile nature of love born from desperation, of connection forged in the fires of rebound. What had once seemed like a refuge from the storms of life now became a battleground   a battleground where dreams clashed with reality, where hope wilted in the face of disillusionment.

Like so many others, I ignored the red flags, warning signs and even God, and moved forward into a marriage that I knew was doomed from the start. On the outside, we looked like a picture-perfect couple. Inside our home, however, was quite the opposite. Soon after the honeymoon was over, my new husband received a promotion, and we bought a house. Our schedules had been upended by his new position, causing us to now see one another only in passing. Now working the night shift and I, still working during the day, created a rift in our relationship that we were not prepared to deal with so early in our marriage. What I had become accustomed to was no longer my reality. I found myself in a new home lonely and alone every day and every night, even on his days off.

While dealing with life as it were, one day I received a phone call while out with a friend. The voice on the other end of the line communicated that my mother had given him my number and told him to call and inform me that he was my biological father. As the story goes, after seeing my mother on a public city bus that he was driving, my real father inquired about me, and she told him in a brief conversation that it was time that I finally knew the truth. Forty-one years prior, during the time that my mom and dad had broken up and were separated, my mother met my biological father and spent some time together. After she discovered that she was pregnant, she informed my biological father who was only home for a brief time, while serving in the Navy. She wanted to get married, but he said that he was not ready to be a husband and father. He left town and went back to the naval base. My mom, pregnant and alone, went back to my dad and told him that she was carrying his child. The revelation shattered the illusion of certainty that had defined my existence for over four decades. After 41 years, the truth emerged which had been covered by deceit and betrayal. The discovery shook the very foundations of my identity. For years, I had navigated life with a sense of belonging, a sense of connection to the man I had called daddy, unaware of the tangled web of lies and deception that lay hidden beneath the surface. Forty-one years later, the past finally caught up with my father after seeing my mother. He explained that he had called me once before, fifteen years prior. With my mother being a crack addict at the time, I didn't believe him and just thought he was trying to get money out of her which was not unusual. I was also going through a divorce and not in an emotional or mental space to receive what he was saying during the call that only lasted a few minutes, so I told him that I had a father and to never call me again. And he didn't, until now.

While on the call this time around, he shared that he had followed my life as I grew up and knew all about me and my family. He said he even knew my pastor and wanted to meet me, so I suggested meeting in my pastor's office where I would feel safe. As I stood face to face with my biological father, during our introduction he suggested that it was my mother who requested that he not interfere and tell me the truth because she told my dad that I was his child. I asked for a DNA test for proof of his claim, although after seeing him for the first time, I already had it. It was like looking in a mirror! The questions I had always had about my height and my small nose had been answered in an instant. DNA testing became more than just a scientific endeavor, it became a journey of self-discovery, a quest for truth. With each swab, my mind filled with questions and my heart with fear and anxiety. The test was conclusive and showed that in fact I did carry his DNA and he was indeed my father. I can only convey and articulate what happened in the weeks and months to follow as life-altering and traumatic. Discovering that my identity was built on a lie was soul crushing. It ripped off all the emotional band aids that I had in place covering my feelings of abandonment and rejection from my dad. Now knowing that my real father knew about my existence from the beginning but made a conscious decision to not be a part of my life, only to marry another woman and start a new family a few years later broke a piece of me that only God would be able to repair. I felt so unwanted and unloved. In the months to come, seeing him and his family was a constant reminder that he threw me away no matter how much he blamed my mother for his decision. The presence of his wife and children served as a stark reminder of the life he had built in my absence.

Navigating my feelings during our times of reunion, I found myself grappling with overwhelming emotions of abandonment and isolation. Developing a relationship with him became more than just a journey, it became a pilgrimage to the heart of my own identity, a quest for understanding who I really was. As I attempted to reconcile and accept the truth of my identity, one evening at a ball game, while sitting on his motorcycle, I asked him to take a picture of me with my phone. I liked the idea of sitting but my fear would keep me from ever riding the bike. Later that evening I posted the picture on social media with the caption that read "posing on my daddy's bike," While in bed asleep, lying next to my husband, I received a call that night from my father's daughters (my sisters) asking me to remove the post from social media because it was hurtful to see that I called him daddy in the post and their family was having a difficult time with it. And as painful as that phone call was, it was a clear reminder of the truth, which is that we were only related by blood, but we were not family. As I navigated the reconciliation, I carried with me the scars of abandonment. From year to year, with every attempt, I never felt like I was a part of the family and belonged, but rather an awkward bystander and outcast. I eventually stopped trying to fit into the puzzle that I didn't belong to.

Not only was I dealing with emotional pain but physical as well. After years of appointments to the doctor for back pain and just being prescribed pain medication, it was not until I visited a new chiropractor that I finally received a proper diagnosis. Through careful review of x-rays and physical manipulation, he discovered that I had scoliosis with a severe curvature of the spine. Not only that, but I also had degenerative disc disease, several herniated spinal discs, and degenerative osteoarthritis. I was referred to an orthopedic surgeon who suggested back surgery. Within weeks, I had to undergo laser surgery to remove bone spurs from my spine, a facet ablation and a spinal laminectomy. Grateful to God, I survived the surgery, and painful recovery, and was able to return to my normal activities and experience a better quality of life physically.

As the years rolled on in my marriage, we continued to look happy in front of family and friends. In public and at family gatherings and holiday parties, we were a happy couple. Behind closed doors we were only business partners managing the business of our home. When my husband was home, he stayed in the basement which was his man cave that I called "Apartment B," playing video games on the internet with gaming friends in other cities, wearing headphones, while I spent my time upstairs in Apartment A.

While this created some tension in the home, there were many other things that contributed to the failure of our marriage. Now understanding that Quality Time is my love language, and this was like a foreign language in our home, it led to look for other ways to fill my time. When my daughter would come home from college and eventually move back home after graduation, I spent my time with her, beginning my journey toward a healthy lifestyle by better food choices and more exercise. When my son and his girlfriend gave me my first grandchild, I allowed them to move into our home, which caused a major disruption and was detrimental to our relationship. I made the selfish decision against my husband's wishes out of my own bitterness and loneliness. I enjoyed having people in the house again, now that my children were working adults, and the blessing of the grandbaby brought a joy that I'd never known before. But the happy times were also difficult ones as the hostility between my son and husband was always present and eventually erupted. Leading to another physical altercation, this would create a fissure in the relationship between me and my son for the next decade.

Our inability to communicate about the issues in our home led my husband to seek validation, approval, and encouragement, elsewhere, often from women. His so-called friendships for support became emotional affairs which eventually led to physical marital infidelity. In the throes of conflict, we sought allies, friends, and family drawn into the vortex of our dysfunction, forced to take sides in a battle that no one could win. Mistrust became more than just a feeling, it was a constant companion, a shadow that followed us wherever we went, poisoning the wellspring of our affection with its bitter touch. Each glance became a question, each word a potential weapon in the arsenal of suspicion that threatened to tear us apart. In the aftermath of betrayal, I grappled with a myriad of emotions from anger and sorrow to disbelief and despair.

When his hard work and desire to become a DJ paid off and was no longer just a dream, what we thought would save our marriage and bring us closer together eventually ripped us apart. The allure of fame and fortune, juxtaposed against the obligations and responsibilities of family life, created a profound fracture between us. As the spotlight and the music called his name, the distance between us widened, a gaping chasm of unspoken desires and unmet expectations that threatened to consume the fragile bond of our marriage.

In the glow of the club lights, the admiration of strangers exceeded the quiet joys of home and family. Each beat of the music became a siren's call, pulling him further from the warmth of our embrace, further from the love that once defined us. As his star ascended, so did the distance between us, a void that widened with each passing day. For him, the drug of fame and fortune was intoxicating. But for me, it was a prison, a cage that held me captive, bound by the chains of unfulfilled dreams and shattered expectations. In the silence of the night, I grappled with the harsh truths of our reality, the bitter taste of loneliness, the sting of abandonment, the ache of a heart that longed for connection. Although I had every material possession I had ever dreamed of, a big house, cars in the driveway, closets filled with clothes and fur coats, and a big diamond on my finger, stress and anxiety filled my days while I lay in a cold bed alone at night, which became a testament to the price we paid for his success, a price measured in tears shed and moments lost.

The evil from his addiction exploded one night when I confronted him outside of the nightclub where he was playing about another woman that he'd been seen with. The rage that I saw in his eyes can only be described as demonic. As I walked away from our confrontation, he grabbed me by the arm pulling me back to him. I pulled away again trying to free myself from his grasp, running to safety in my friend's car. He pursued in a chase and before I could get in the car to close the door, he attempted to snatch my phone from my hand to see the proof of what I had been told earlier that day. We fought for my phone, and I finally won the battle to get it back, but not the war. He then reached into the car, and put both hands around by neck, choking me with all his might, attempting to cut off my air supply. Gasping for oxygen, I managed to lift my knees and feet up to his chest to try to push him off me from the front, while my friend got out of the car to pull him off from behind. I could hear her screaming his name and yelling for him to stop. When others around heard and saw what was happening, something in him clicked and he let me go and left.

Our disagreements became the fuel that fed the fires of resentment and discord, a toxic mixture of chaos, unmet expectations and unspoken grievances that poisoned our lives. Each word became a dagger, each accusation a wound that cut deeper than the sharpest blade, leaving behind scars that would never truly heal. Ten years of distance, neglect, and isolation caused mental, physical, and emotional abuse resulting from infidelity with multiple women, strangulation and subsequent emergency protective order, and multiple court appearances. Our marriage finally hit the breaking point. The corrosive effects of constant arguments, disagreements, and physical altercations exacerbated by the growing divide in priorities and lifestyles, led us down the painful path of divorce. The decision to file for divorce, though necessary for me, was still very painful. I felt like a failure. Now twice divorced, I was left with misery and regret. Another cup of the bitter taste of loss, the sting of abandonment, the ache of a heart that still longed for love and protection. As I have learned to take lessons from each loss, I acquire more knowledge about myself and what has shaped the woman I am today. After seeking additional therapy and God at a deeper level, God's love and compassion have enabled me to eventually extend forgiveness, grace, and mercy to my ex-husband years later.

"For our struggle is not against flesh and blood, but against the rulers, against the authorities, against the powers of this dark world and against the spiritual forces of evil in the heavenly realms." Ephesians 6:12 (NIV)

Chapter 5.

Suffering in Pain

The transition after my divorce from the familiar confines of a shared home to the solitary confines of a small apartment, compounded by the solitude brought about by the COVID-19 pandemic, evoked dire feelings of loneliness and despair. All alone in the quiet solitude of my small one-bedroom apartment, the weight of isolation bore down upon me, a heavy burden that threatened to crush the fragile remnants of my shattered heart. The COVID-19 pandemic, with its mandates of social distancing and self-isolation, only served to worsen the sense of bleakness that consumed me. A relentless tide of isolation swept away the remnants of normalcy, leaving behind a landscape devoid of human connection.

Now working from home since I was not an essential worker and alone with my thoughts, I wrestled with the harsh reality of my newfound solitude. Each moment became a monument to the absence of companionship, friendship, and family bonds. Had it not been for the lifeline and anchor of my faith in God and His word, I would have crossed the thin line from sanity to insanity on more than one occasion. I'm sure the neighbors above my head heard the countless nights that I cried out to God in agony wondering if the pain and anguish I felt on the inside would ever dissipate.

As the days turned into weeks, and the weeks into months, I forged a new relationship with myself — a journey of self-discovery and self-acceptance born from the ashes of loss and despair. In the seclusion of my apartment, I found the beauty of a sunset viewed through the window of my confinement. The bunny rabbits that would run up to my patio door filled me with joy. Watching the neighbors walk their dogs and play fetch in the field behind me brought me much pleasure.

As the death toll began to rise across the country and the realization of how precious life really is set in, I gained strength to emerge from the emptiness of my world and grab hold of life outside the walls of my apartment. I began to take drives in the car with the windows down, sun on my face, wind in my hair, the music blaring, singing along to my favorite songs. Donned in my facial mask covering my nose and mouth, I started taking daily walks in the nearby park and feeding the ducks in the ponds. I took my loneliness and despair outside and gave it to the wind in exchange for the joy of the Lord and a heart filled with gratitude for me and my family living to see another day. Even though my family was all touched by COVID at some point, some worse than others, some more than once even after being vaccinated, I'm so thankful that we all survived, although my symptoms of a headache, sore throat, nausea and vomiting, loss of appetite, dizziness, an extreme exhaustion felt like I was at death's door.

As the use of technology soared during COVID, I learned more about Zoom, YouTube, Netflix, social media, and dating apps than ever before. Learning new information and skills like crocheting my own hair, mastering different line dances that I never knew existed, and making new dishes from recipes found online helped pass the time. I also began to study wealth creation, money management, and investment principles, credit repair, debt reduction strategies and savings tips and tools that helped me raise my credit score from 500 to over 760. A new sisterhood of friends was birthed from the seclusion, and we named ourselves the Quarantine Queens. My friends and I had movie dates, played games, and took shots on Zoom and the Messenger app. We would meet in a park and the field behind my apartment, sit six feet apart wearing our masks, bringing a meal and breaking bread together as we shared our personal experiences of how we were surviving in our own bubbles at home. With all the houses of worship being closed, including my own, I found new churches on Facebook and YouTube and began tuning in to creative home services and Bible studies across the country. My hope in God is the only thing that got me through that period of my life. My faith in the promises of His word kept me hanging on, believing that a better day was coming.

As the world opened back up so did my single life. From the dating profiles created during the quarantine, and after all the late-night conversations, it was time to put an actual face with a name and the voice on the other end of the phone. What came next was an endless stream of first dates from the dizzying whirl of dating sites and the frenetic energy of parties. Going to every promoter's party hoping to find Mr. Right or Mr. Right Now, and despite being inebriated every weekend from rum and bourbon leaving behind pounding migraines and hangovers the next morning, believing it would suppress my feelings of loneliness, I still found myself adrift in a sea of superficial connections, longing for something more, something deeper than the transient pleasures of the night. For years, I chased the elusive mirage of fulfillment. Degrading myself, accepting treatment that I knew I didn't deserve and was worthy of much more, the chemicals and neurotransmitters of dopamine, oxytocin, and norepinephrine kept me going back to the same detrimental behavior. Jumping in and out of bed with men that I didn't know, holding on to inconsistent actions and meaningless promises, all the while feeling broken and ashamed. And yet, with each fleeting encounter, and each hollow exchange, the emptiness within me only seemed to grow, a gaping void that threatened to swallow me whole. I began living a life that was contrary to everything I believed in. I became the very thing that had damaged my relationships and destroyed my marriages. I became untrustworthy by lying. I became unfaithful by not keeping my word. I became emotionally abusive by taking advantage of men and intentionally hurting their feelings which gave me a sense of control. I avoided attachments and kept my distance between me and others so that they would not see the pain that I was feeling inside, preventing me from being hurt again. Yes, hurt people really do hurt other people.

After surviving COVID19 and using the wisdom I had gained to put into practice everything I had learned to position myself for my next chapter of life, I found myself better off than before. With a new title and promotion, stronger faith, more hope, and greater anticipation about the future, God blessed me with a bright future in a beautiful new house that I could call my own. As I stepped onto the threshold of my new, beautiful oasis, gratitude washed over me. I was still in disbelief that after the pain and trauma of what I had suffered just three years prior, and for all my sinful behavior, God would still show me favor and bless me with my new home. And yet, beneath the surface of my gratitude lay a current of apprehension and fear. For while I was thankful for the abundance that surrounded me, I couldn't shake the feeling of being overwhelmed, the sense that I had bitten off more than I could chew, that the weight of responsibility was more than I could bear alone. In the quiet moments all alone, I surveyed the vast expanse of my new home, I felt the enormity of the task before me, a mountain of chores and responsibilities that loomed large on the horizon. From the mundane tasks of household maintenance to the financial burdens of homeownership, I found myself grappling with the reality of my new circumstances that demanded more of me than I had ever been asked to give and stretched me beyond the limits of my comfort zone.

And as I settled into my new home, I learned to lean into the discomfort, to embrace the challenges as opportunities for growth and transformation. With each passing day, I discovered strength within myself that I never knew existed. I began to realize that while my new home may have been more than I bargained for, it was also a symbol of possibility, of endless potential waiting to be unlocked. And as I stood in the sanctuary of my sunroom, looking out into the big backyard, fishpond, and swimming pool, I knew that I was exactly where I was meant to be. With gratitude in my heart, I opened the doors of my home to family and friends, welcoming them in, creating shared laughter and cherished memories. Together, we forged new bonds of friendship and kinship. In the moments of fellowship, amidst the laughter and joy that filled the air, I was overcome with delight from the simple pleasures of reminiscing about stories of memories, playing with my grandchildren and dogs in the yard, the smoke rising from the barbeque grill, music filling the air, the water splashing out of the pool, the screaming children sliding from the inflatable house, all while I prepared meals with enough food to feed an army. Being together for the holidays, birthdays, and parties for every occasion, was an unspoken language of love that bound us together as one family.

After the parties were over, the guests were gone, and the kitchen was cleaned, I still felt the weight of loneliness throughout the dark, empty rooms. Despite the abundance of space and comfort that surrounded me, I couldn't shake the feeling of emptiness — the longing for a partner to enjoy it all with, a companion to build memories and dreams with. I found myself returning to the familiar embrace of dating apps in search of the potential for genuine connection in the digital world brimming with possibility, yet full of uncertainty. As I navigated the virtual realm of online dating once again, I braced myself for the highs and lows of human connection. With each swipe, I swam out into uncharted water, hoping against hope that somewhere amidst the sea of profiles and pictures, I would find the one. With the excitement from messages and calls only lasting a few days to a week, the harsh reality of modern dating was emotionally draining with superficiality, games, ghosting, psycho-stalker drama, the constant pressure to present myself in the most flattering light and position, and cropping every picture to cut what would surely appear to be unflattering excess weight in my eyes. As I swiped and scrolled, I held onto the belief that there existed the possibility for magic and that love would find its way to me. But again, disappointment, inconsistency, lies, and broken promises left me dismayed. No amount of partying, alcohol, or sex could fill the hole in my heart. I was weary, tired, and sad. Some days I didn't want to get out of bed, so I didn't. I would lie there, day after day, crying as the tears soaked my pillow, asking God when it would all be over. But in true form of doing what

I've always done, I put on a smile and held onto the only thing I knew — my faith in God. I kept moving. I didn't give up, even on the days that I wanted to.

"To all who mourn in Israel, he will give a crown of beauty for ashes, a joyous blessing instead of mourning, festive praise instead of despair. In their righteousness, they will be like great oaks that the Lord has planted for his own glory." Isaiah 61:3 (NLT)

Chapter 6.

Healed of Pain

Being raised by my grandmother and going to church all my life, my existence centered around my family and church. That's all I knew. It was my identity. I have sung in the choir in every church that I've ever attended. I've worked in ministry as a Sunday school teacher, usher, greeter, women's ministry leader, committee chairperson, cooked in the kitchen and even cleaned bathrooms. My grandmother was the epitome of a servant of the Lord and whatever needed to be done, she did. Likewise, it was no wonder that I was of the same mindset. Having been in the same city most of my life and a member of several large churches, not only had I never attended this one, but I had never heard of it nor the pastor. I met the first lady when she was referred to me during my divorce, after putting my house up for sale. She mentioned her church in conversation and invited me to visit. I accepted her offer, and I'm so thankful that I did!

At my lowest point, I would come in the front doors of the church, sit in the corner of the very last row, and weep throughout the service, then quietly slip out at the end. The presence of the Lord kept me coming back. I felt a gentle peace there. From the very beginning, MOC felt like home. At Ministries of Christ, I found more than just a church, I found a family, and a community united by a shared commitment to love and service. Here, amidst the warmth of fellowship and the embrace of divine grace, I discovered a sense of belonging that resonated deep within my soul. In the company of like-minded believers, kindred spirits, and fellow seekers of the Gospel of Truth, I found peace, through shared prayers, in the harmony of voices lifted in praise, and in worship that bound us together as one body, one family in Christ. With each passing Sunday, as I gathered with my brothers and sisters in faith, I felt the presence of the Holy Spirit and the gentle whisper of divine guidance, leading me along the path of righteousness and service.

It was a small congregation compared to what I was used to, not more than seventy-five people on most Sundays. Although they were small in number, the praise and worship to God was incredible. The hearts of the people were very generous in their community outreach efforts of providing free meals to the community each week, clothing giveaways, back to school backpacks, winter coats for children, and annual fall community festival. It felt so good to be connected to a community of believers whose main mission was to make life better for others. I knew this was where I was supposed to be in this season of my life. I needed to believe in a vision and place my time and energy into something bigger than myself. The Holy Bible states in Proverbs 18:16 NKJV "A man's gift makes room for him and brings him before great men."

God allowed the leadership of the ministry to see something in me that I didn't even see in myself. Discovering a spiritual home and community where I could use my gifts and talents to serve others and honor the Lord was a profound and fulfilling journey. So as God would have it, I began serving in ministry on the praise team, the communications and marketing team as the Director of Communications, working with new members in our Foundations class, the greeters and security team as Connections Ministry Director, and various other committees even being ordained as a Deaconess. I was a faithful servant to the ministry and the Lord Jesus Christ, and my life was once again filled with passion by helping others.

As I sought the presence of the Lord, he began to heal my wounds and transform my mind. I found myself sitting all alone in my quiet home contemplating the state of my existence. Now twice divorced, with two adult children living on their own, and a grandmother of two beautiful girls, I just knew there had to be more to the rest of my life. While on the outside to others, my life seemed full and complete. I was always doing something. Hosting parties for family and friends, going to community events with my sister-friends, planning the weekly WDW also known as Wind Down Wednesday dinner, coordinating Quarantine Queens social gatherings, traveling around the country, counseling young women, and serving in ministry at my church throughout the week, all while working 40 to 50 hours per week on my job after 27 years of service to the same company. Indeed, I was busy. I was told things like "I love watching you live your life," and "I'm living vicariously through you," and "I want to be just like you when I grow up," and "I don't know how you do it, you have the energy of a thirty-year old." Whew! — if they only knew. I had lived my entire adult life consumed by the roles of a wife and mother since I was 19 years old. My life consisted of working, cooking, cleaning, taking care of my family, and serving in ministry at church. That was my existence for more than 30 years. That's all I knew, and my life made sense. I was complete. Until I wasn't.

Like so many others, I was living a double life. Although I was going to church and faithfully serving in ministry every week, I was exhausted. I was still "living my best life" with my friends and family. They knew that "the church girl" had a curfew on Saturday night no matter what was going on, and even if the party was at my house, but I was still burned out from the partying. I had dating fatigue from talking to one new man after the next every couple of months on the dating apps. I was drained from making decisions for others and having all the answers all the time. I was weary from carrying my concerns and disappointments along with everyone else's. I was just plain ole tired and needed rest! I needed to rest my mind, my body, and my soul. I had come to a point where I just wanted to lay it all down at the feet of Jesus and tell Him

"Ok, I give up, I can't do it anymore," and what I found was that's exactly where He wanted me to be. At the end of the summer parties, after my last summer vacation to Jamaica, as the season began to change, so did I. Something was different this year. The things that used to bring me joy and fill my calendar and my heart left me dissatisfied and wanting more. I began to feel a void that could not be filled no matter how many people were in the room. This void and expanse in my soul kept widening when SUDDENLY one day I felt the presence of God like never before and the Holy Spirit led me to a spiritual fast. I had the strongest desire to draw away from everyone and everything to become still and quiet so that I could hear from God.

He had been waiting for me to come to a place of total surrender so that I could finally hear Him, but it was in this place of surrender that I also gave Him my consecrated heart, complete obedience, and the YES he had been longing to hear.

YES to doing it His way and not my own.

YES to serving Him first and not everyone else.

YES to putting Him first and not my own wants and needs.

YES to doing what He wanted me to do and not what my flesh wanted to do.

YES to pursuing His desires for my life and not my own selfish desires.

YES to praying for His will for my life and not what I thought I wanted.

YES to living my life to fulfill the purpose for which I was created and not just existing from day to day to fulfill my need for instant gratification.

I answered the call in my spirit and gave God 21 days of consecration and cleansing. In the act of complete surrender, I gave up everything that kept me from his heavenly presence. For three weeks I devoted myself to prayer, studying God's word, and praise and worship. I ate only fruit and vegetables and only drank water, natural fruit juices, and natural tea. During this time, I found liberation and embraced the truth of my own imperfections and surrendered them to the mercy of a loving God. It was a surrender that transcended the limitations of my own understanding. He began to speak to me in ways I had never experienced before. As I relinquished control and entrusted my life to the hands of my Creator, I felt a profound sense of peace over me, that surpassed all understanding, anchoring me in the unshakeable foundation of faith. God began to show up in ways that were undeniable. I began to see visions for my life that I hadn't seen before. As I prayed asking him to connect me with people who could help me bring the vision to pass, He answered my prayers by bringing people into my life that I would not ordinarily meet for any reason at all. Within the first 10 days of the consecration, God had revealed to me what my mission was to be.

In surrender, I found purpose. A purpose rooted in service, in love, in the relentless pursuit of truth and righteousness. It was a purpose that illuminated the path before me, guiding me toward a life defined not by the pleasures of the world, but by my love for God and sacrificial offering of gratitude. And so, with a grateful heart and a spirit renewed, I embarked on the next chapter of my journey, *to guide others to LOVE, with LOVE, from LOVE; for God is LOVE.*

In that moment, I was reborn in the image of God. Reborn in the likeness of my heavenly Creator, not in the likeness of culture. Reborn, with the mind of Christ, not the mind of people around me. Reborn with the Holy Spirit, not the demonic spirits that had been influencing my life. I died to my fleshly desires. I died to giving into the pleasures of the world. I died to believing the lies of the devil. I died to doing things my way so that I could truly live the abundant life of Christ by doing things his way. I died. I died so that I could be reborn.

"Whoever is a believer in Christ is a new creation. The old way of living has disappeared. A new way of living has come into existence." 2 Corinthians 5:17 (GW)

Chapter 7.

Purposed Fulfilled

While on my spiritual quest for purpose, I began to hear God so clearly. My spirit was open and eager to receive every word, precept, and promise of God. It wasn't until I was in the very presence of my Creator, seeing His face through my praise and worship, in spirit and in truth, was my life's mission revealed. Until that time, I did not believe that my story of survival and transformation was worth sharing. Along with answering YES to God's will and purpose for my life, I also gave Him a YES to tell the world how unbelievably loving, forgiving, faithful, patient, kind, compassionate, merciful, and REAL He truly is. With courage and determination, I embarked on a new chapter of my life defined by purpose and passion.

When I finally laid down my life at the feet of Jesus and allowed the Holy Spirit to take full of control of it, I began to finally see me through the lens of my Heavenly Father. My entire mindset began to shift. The negative thoughts, feelings, emotions and behaviors that had taken root, shaping my attitude and belief system had been exposed, uprooted and thrown into the fire so that I could be purified. One by one, God began to remove the weeds of fear, bitterness, anger, distrust, guilt, and shame. As I gave my heart to Him, He gave me His strength, peace, comfort, contentment, and filled me with faith. Faith to trust him and others again. Faith to believe that there was more life for me to live. The abundant life that Jesus died for me to have. So I took the Lord's hand and never looked back.

During those 21 days of prayer with a consecrated heart, God not only heard but answered every prayer concerning my new mission in life. I knew that the task was far too great of an undertaking for me to accomplish alone. I prayed for wisdom to apply all of the knowledge that I had gained through the years that could equip and empower others. I prayed for a mentor and coach to help me align my steps with the vision. I prayed that God would connect me with people and resources to make provision and bring it to pass. I prayed that he would lead those to me that would benefit from what he was calling me to do.

And as I look back on the journey that brought me to this moment, I marveled at the beauty of God's plan, at the miracles that unfolded when I surrendered to His will. Not realizing that he had been ordering my steps the entire time, I had already begun the process of preparing without knowing it. Earlier that year, I had registered to attend a business conference as an investment for personal growth. My desire was to become more knowledgeable about investments and gain tools to build my own financial portfolio. Little did I know, God had a different plan. I did not leave the conference with the financial competence that I had hoped for but took with me something far more valuable. A new mindset in the way I viewed my own self-worth. I now believed that God saw value in me and that I had something valuable to offer others. God also answered my prayer and connected me with my mentor and coach, who I will forever be grateful for. She helped me to evolve and become the Kingdom woman of God and businesswoman that I am today. God began to expand the vision and allowed me to see it through His eyes. And thus, She Is Me Ministry was born.

She Is Me, a simple yet profound declaration of identity is a testament to the power of sisterhood and solidarity. Accepting this clarion call, I became a voice that spoke truth to power, that championed the cause of justice and equality, that celebrated the beauty and resilience of womanhood in all its forms. She Is Me was the fulfillment of my entire life's journey, equipping and empowering Sisters. Hurting. Everywhere to become Sisters. Healed. Everywhere. With each class, and each act of love and service, I found fulfillment in the knowledge that I was walking in alignment with my divine purpose. And as I shared my gifts and talents with others, as I stood shoulder to shoulder with my sisters in faith, I felt the presence of God.

Through deliverance and surrender, allowing God to change my mind and my life, I am now walking in purpose to fulfill my spiritual destiny. With each step, guided by the Holy Spirit, I embraced the calling on my life, born from the depths of my own suffering to lead other hurting women through their life's experiences to find redemption, transformation, healing, and restoration. I have found in the company of wounded souls and broken spirits, and through the shared stories of pain and triumph, there is the sacred bond that unites us as sisters in spirit and purpose. In the ministry of redemption and restoration, I have sought to be a vessel of divine love, and a conduit through which the healing power of God can flow, bringing hope and renewal to those who have been broken by the storms of life. With each word spoken, each hand extended in love, I witness before my eye's miracles of transformation, healing, and restoration, as broken hearts are mended and wounded spirits find comfort and strength.

"Many plans are in a man's mind, But it is the Lord's purpose for him that will stand (be carried out)."

Proverbs 19:21 (AMP)

Chapter 8.

The Blueprint

During the construction phases of my life, God used the building blocks of my pain to erect a masterpiece of purpose: my Creator's divine design, born from the depths of my own suffering, and illuminated by the light of His grace. Through the twists and turns of my life's journey, I discovered that my pain was not merely a burden to bear, but a pathway to redemption, a roadmap to transformation. Through adversity, there were bits and pieces of God's plan for my purpose, connecting one with another. With each trial and tribulation, with each moment of despair and doubt, the hand of God was guiding me, shaping me, molding me into the vessel He had always intended me to be.

As I journeyed through the valley of the shadow of death, I discovered that my pain was not a curse, but a blessing in disguise by a loving God who saw beyond my brokenness to the beauty that lay beneath. And so, with a heart full of gratitude and a spirit renewed, I embraced my purpose for which I had been created, the purpose for which I had been redeemed. Through the power of my testimony, through the beauty of my brokenness, I became a living testament to the transformative power of God's love and a beacon of light and hope in a dark world.

With each step forward, guided by the hand of God, I walked the path of redemption, knowing that my pain had not been in vain, but had been sanctified by the touch of divine grace. And as I shared my story with the world, I became a vessel of hope, a messenger of love, a living testament to the power of transformation that lies within us all.

In the blueprint of my pain, God revealed the purpose of my life — to be a witness to His boundless love, to be a beacon of hope in a world desperate for redemption, to show others the way to transformation through the power of my own life's journey.

While my memoir does not include every detail and experience of my life, it does serve as a testament to highlight the transformative power of divine grace and is a tribute to the beauty of redemption and purpose found during pain and suffering. As I have shared my story with you, may these words and biblical truths inspire you to embrace your own journey of transformation, knowing that in the hands of a loving God, all things are possible, and miracles do happen each and every day!

SHE IS ME MINISTRY

"Empowering women to accept the PAST, create the

FUTURE, by preparing TODAY."

https://sheismeministry.com

SHE IS ME MINISTRY Mission Statement

SHE IS ME MINISTRY will nurture, empower, and care for underprivileged, impoverished, and disenfranchised SISTERS. HURTING. EVERYWHERE; to be restored from their point of brokenness spiritually, mentally, physically, emotionally, and financially to a life of wholeness. We seek to create an environment that will promote a desire of healthy growth that will guide women back to a path of successful living. The aim of SHE IS ME MINISTRY is to transform women's lives and strengthen families by applying biblical principles for living with unconditional love for the whole person.

SHE IS ME MINISTRY Vision Statement

Our aim is to guide women in discovering and accessing various key principles, tools, and skills that will bring about healing and restoration to replace brokenness and disappointment. We hope to instill the belief that you can live a life with vision and on purpose, full of peace, joy and prosperity.

SHE IS ME is a ministry composed of a team of committed women who desire to make a positive impact in the world. As we build relationships of trust during our quarterly 12-week course, we purpose to share the love of Jesus Christ by offering hope. We facilitate a thought-provoking discussion in each weekly two-hour session, using the structured Heavenly Images Curriculum found in "A Journey of Transformation" by Tracey Bradley, which addresses the mindset and life skills development, establishes strategies for success by using resources and experts in the community, monitors progress, and offers incentives for completion of goals. The ministry also hosts a monthly Purpose and Power Potluck which provides an atmosphere for honest dialogue and community connection to create plans and strategies for building a better world today as well as the future generations. Through educational materials, seminars, retreats, and conferences, our goal is to equip and empower others to become healthy, wealthy, and whole in every area of their lives.

Heavenly Images Curriculum

Phase 1: The Mindset

Romans 12:2

"Do not conform any longer to the pattern of this world but be transformed by the renewing of your mind. Then you will be able to test and approve what God's will is — His good, pleasing, and perfect will."

- Love Yourself — 1 John 4:8, Psalm 139:13–16
- Know Yourself — Ephesians 4:22–24
- Spiritual Warfare — Ephesians 6:11–18
- Living Victoriously- Colossians 2:15
- Healthy Start — 1 Corinthians 6:19–20
- Positive Language and Etiquette — Colossians 3:17

Phase 2: Life Skills

Hosea 4:6, Deuteronomy 8:18

My people are destroyed from lack of knowledge.

But remember the Lord your God, for it is he who gives you the ability to produce wealth.

- Time Management — Proverbs 10:4

- Career Development — Proverbs 14:23

- Wealth Management — Deuteronomy 8:18

- Leaving a Legacy (Estate Planning) — Proverbs 13:22

- Vision and Purpose — Philippians 4:13

- Completion Celebration

** Find this course in "A Journey of Transformation" by Tracey Bradley**

About the Author

Recognized as one of the most empowering, engaging, and enthusiastic voices in women's empowerment, Tracey Bradley, a passionate advocate for spiritual growth, is a dynamic speaker and founder of She Is Me Ministry. With a profound commitment to inspiring and uplifting women, Tracey Bradley brings a wealth of experience and a genuine spirit of compassion to her ministry.

With a background of more than two decades as a Christian leader, teacher, minister, spiritual advisor, deaconess, and prison mentor, Tracey has dedicated her life to serving and empowering women on their journeys of self-discovery and spiritual fulfillment. Her expertise lies in using fundamental principles and key life skills to transform lives and create a better future for families and communities. She is also a social advocate, having led and participated in several non-violent demonstrations including most recently, the 2020

March in Washington DC, where she is featured in a *National Geographic* article.

As the visionary behind the She Is Me Ministry, Tracey has created a sacred movement for women to connect, grow, and find strength in their shared experiences. The ministry focuses on a complete framework for holistic healing and recovery, teaching fundamental principles and key life skills through a structured curriculum that will transform lives and create a better future for families and future generations. Tracey's transformational principles impact audiences, so they learn to embrace greatness and achieve success. Her dynamic expertise has earned her invitations to speak at women's conferences and on powerful stages like the Broken, Bound, but Becoming Healing Summit hosted by Brandy Nicole.

Made in the USA
Columbia, SC
13 June 2024

36568738R40078